My Time With GOD In Prayer

A Prayer Journal For Women

ACTIVINOTES

Activinotes

DAILY JOURNALS, PLANNERS, NOTEBOOKS AND OTHER BLANK BOOKS

All Rights reserved. No part of this book may be reproduced or used in any way or form or by any means whether electronic or mechanical, this means that you cannot record or photocopy any material ideas or tips that are provided in this book.

Copyright 2016

Emergency Numbers:

When in sorrow, call John 14
When men fail you, call Psalm 27
When you have sinned, call Psalm 51
When you worry, call Matthew 6:19-34
When you are in danger, call Psalm 91
When God seems far away, call Psalm 139
When your faith needs stirring, call Hebrew 11
When you are lonely and fearful, call Psalm 23
When you grow bitter and critical, call 1 Cor. 13
When you feel down and out, call Romans 8:31-39
When you want peace and rest, call Matthews 11:25-30
When the world seems bigger than God, call Psalm 90
When you leave home for labor or travel, call Psalm 121
When youre prayers grow narrow or selfish, call Psalm 67

Date:

Scripture for the day:

What should I pray for today?

Who should I pray for?

How can I make my prayer become more meaningful?

Date:

Scripture for the day:

What should I pray for today?

Who should I pray for?

How can I make my prayer become more meaningful?

Date:

Scripture for the day:

What should I pray for today?

Who should I pray for?

How can I make my prayer become more meaningful?

Date:

Scripture for the day:

What should I pray for today?

Who should I pray for?

How can I make my prayer become more meaningful?

Date:

Scripture for the day:

What should I pray for today?

Who should I pray for?

How can I make my prayer become more meaningful?

Date:

Scripture for the day:

What should I pray for today?

Who should I pray for?

How can I make my prayer become more meaningful?

Date:

Scripture for the day:

What should I pray for today?

Who should I pray for?

How can I make my prayer become more meaningful?

Date:

Scripture for the day:

What should I pray for today?

Who should I pray for?

How can I make my prayer become more meaningful?

Date:

Scripture for the day:

What should I pray for today?

Who should I pray for?

How can I make my prayer become more meaningful?

Date:

Scripture for the day:

What should I pray for today?

Who should I pray for?

How can I make my prayer become more meaningful?

Date:

Scripture for the day:

What should I pray for today?

Who should I pray for?

How can I make my prayer become more meaningful?

Date:

Scripture for the day:

What should I pray for today?

Who should I pray for?

How can I make my prayer become more meaningful?

Date:

Scripture for the day:

What should I pray for today?

Who should I pray for?

How can I make my prayer become more meaningful?

Date:

Scripture for the day:

What should I pray for today?

Who should I pray for?

How can I make my prayer become more meaningful?

Date:

Scripture for the day:

What should I pray for today?

Who should I pray for?

How can I make my prayer become more meaningful?

Date:

Scripture for the day:

What should I pray for today?

Who should I pray for?

How can I make my prayer become more meaningful?

Date:

Scripture for the day:

What should I pray for today?

Who should I pray for?

How can I make my prayer become more meaningful?

Date:

Scripture for the day:

What should I pray for today?

Who should I pray for?

How can I make my prayer become more meaningful?

Date:

Scripture for the day:

What should I pray for today?

Who should I pray for?

How can I make my prayer become more meaningful?

Date:

Scripture for the day:

What should I pray for today?

Who should I pray for?

How can I make my prayer become more meaningful?

Date:

Scripture for the day:

What should I pray for today?

Who should I pray for?

How can I make my prayer become more meaningful?

Date:

Scripture for the day:

What should I pray for today?

Who should I pray for?

How can I make my prayer become more meaningful?

Date:

Scripture for the day:

What should I pray for today?

Who should I pray for?

How can I make my prayer become more meaningful?

Date:

Scripture for the day:

What should I pray for today?

Who should I pray for?

How can I make my prayer become more meaningful?

Date:

Scripture for the day:

What should I pray for today?

Who should I pray for?

How can I make my prayer become more meaningful?

Date:

Scripture for the day:

What should I pray for today?

Who should I pray for?

How can I make my prayer become more meaningful?

Date:

Scripture for the day:

What should I pray for today?

Who should I pray for?

How can I make my prayer become more meaningful?

Date:

Scripture for the day:

What should I pray for today?

Who should I pray for?

How can I make my prayer become more meaningful?

Date:

Scripture for the day:

What should I pray for today?

Who should I pray for?

How can I make my prayer become more meaningful?

Date:

Scripture for the day:

What should I pray for today?

Who should I pray for?

How can I make my prayer become more meaningful?

Date:

Scripture for the day:

What should I pray for today?

Who should I pray for?

How can I make my prayer become more meaningful?

Date:

Scripture for the day:

What should I pray for today?

Who should I pray for?

How can I make my prayer become more meaningful?

Date:

Scripture for the day:

What should I pray for today?

Who should I pray for?

How can I make my prayer become more meaningful?

Date:

Scripture for the day:

What should I pray for today?

Who should I pray for?

How can I make my prayer become more meaningful?

Date:

Scripture for the day:

What should I pray for today?

Who should I pray for?

How can I make my prayer become more meaningful?

Date:

Scripture for the day:

What should I pray for today?

Who should I pray for?

How can I make my prayer become more meaningful?

Date:

Scripture for the day:

What should I pray for today?

Who should I pray for?

How can I make my prayer become more meaningful?

Date:

Scripture for the day:

What should I pray for today?

Who should I pray for?

How can I make my prayer become more meaningful?

Date:

Scripture for the day:

What should I pray for today?

Who should I pray for?

How can I make my prayer become more meaningful?

Date:

Scripture for the day:

What should I pray for today?

Who should I pray for?

How can I make my prayer become more meaningful?

Date:

Scripture for the day:

What should I pray for today?

Who should I pray for?

....

....

....

....

How can I make my prayer become more meaningful?

....

....

....

....

....

....

....

....

....

....

....

....

....

....

....

....

....

....

....

....

....

Date:

Scripture for the day:

What should I pray for today?

Who should I pray for?

How can I make my prayer become more meaningful?

Date:

Scripture for the day:

What should I pray for today?

Who should I pray for?

How can I make my prayer become more meaningful?

Date:

Scripture for the day:

What should I pray for today?

Who should I pray for?

How can I make my prayer become more meaningful?

Date:

Scripture for the day:

What should I pray for today?

Who should I pray for?

How can I make my prayer become more meaningful?

Date:

Scripture for the day:

What should I pray for today?

Who should I pray for?

How can I make my prayer become more meaningful?

Date:

Scripture for the day:

What should I pray for today?

Who should I pray for?

How can I make my prayer become more meaningful?

Date:

Scripture for the day:

What should I pray for today?

Who should I pray for?

How can I make my prayer become more meaningful?

Date:

Scripture for the day:

What should I pray for today?

www.ingramcontent.com/pod-product-compliance
Lightning Source LLC
Chambersburg PA
CBHW080739250626
47170CB00010B/2883